TRIUMPH HOUSE

CHRISTIAN VERSE
FROM
NORTHERN IRELAND

Edited by Chris Walton

First published in Great Britain in 1996 by
TRIUMPH HOUSE
1 - 2 Wainman Road, Woodston,
Peterborough, PE2 7BU

HB ISBN 1 86161 020 3
SB ISBN 1 86161 025 4

Foreword

Over one hundred writers from *Northern Ireland* have come together to spread the good word in the form of poetry.

They share their thoughts on the many subjects that make, and mould our lives.

The poems are all connected in some way because each writer has a message to pass on, or a story to tell to the reader.

Many poets hide away their work; at the back of a drawer or in a cupboard - by doing this they are locking their thoughts away.

The *Christian Verse* anthologies act as an important factor in helping us to pass on the Christian Message.

Chris Walton
Editor

CONTENTS

SECRET SEPULCHRE

Can we, on our Easter morn,
Approach with step forlorn
Our own secret sepulchre.
And wonder, if we dare,
What, we will find there?

With loud and hammering heart
Do we find with a start
That the stone is rolled away.
Do we curse, or do we pray?
Is this the providential day?

With pale and sweating face
Do we turn and leave the place,
Turn our back upon our fears
And run with frightened tears
From the terror of the years?

Or with burning anguished tears
Do we set upon our fears,
Enter in the silent tomb
Face the horrors of the room
And confront our deepest doom.

Will we, if we can
See an angel, not a man?
See upon the floor the shroud
And with hope become endowed
Shout our triumph song aloud.

Do we this Easter morn
See our every hope reborn?
Do we put away the pain
See the rainbow - not the rain,
Know the joy of life again?

Lillian E Devlin

MEMORIES

Time, to sit by the fire and reflect
Upon memories stored, for such times
When pain and loneliness begin to crush my spirit
I open the box of memories, deep in my heart and mind

I rummage through such wonders I find
The memory of a sunlit summer's day
A walk on the beach
The smell of salt in the air
And you dear daddy, paddling with me there

A far off memory comes to me
I remember how you would lift and cuddle me
When I would fall, or scrape my knee
Thank you God,
For giving such precious memories to me
They are spiritual medicine
To be taken at times when I feel low
I just sit by the fire, open my heart and mind
and let the joyous memories flow

Linda Andrews

GOD'S KINGDOM

God's Kingdom will be as he promised
A beautiful holy place
A place where Satan can't enter
He won't be assured of a place
Only those with his name on their foreheads
Will be called through the golden gates
No more sorrow or pain we will find there
All worries and cares will be gone.
The tears gently wiped from our eyes.
No wealth of possessions we'll need there
For riches untold will be found.
When at last I look on my saviour
A smile on his gentle face
Surrounded by angels and saints
Around the throne of grace
Their voices sweetly blending
In perfect harmony
Loved ones that have gone before me
Will be waiting there for me
I'm home now at last I am free
So my friend if the broad road you're treading
Just listen a moment to me
My Lord does not want you to perish
All sinners he wants to set free
Just call on his name before it's too late
If God's Kingdom, you want to see
It's now up to you which choice you make.
There's only two ways
The broad or the narrow.

Freda Trimble

THE WONDER OF LOVE

How can a love song pour
Restlessly from a heart
Blackened and scarred,
Sullied by situations past?

How can it be
That love stirs deep,
Bringing joy out of darkness
And wounds to the surface?

How can love be powerless?
How can it lie grey?
At times it only watches
Concern filling its eyes with helpless tears.

How can true love not become action
Prompted by emotion and carried by desire
To leave self-interest behind,
To die having flourished with life?

Martin Walker

REMEMBERING A 'DOWN' DAY

One of my *down* days
I call to mind,
Left alone with
The housework grind.
My family engrossed
With their many cares,
So little time for my affairs.
Life's busy rush
They must obey,
Their many plans
Made for the day.
When ordinary chores
So boring seemed
I thought of what
I might have been.
My intelligence I should have put to the test,
Hold a high position with the best.
Suddenly, peeping through skies of grey
The sun dispelled my gloom away.
I felt the Lord
Was looking down,
Even, on that day
When I wore a frown.
Thanking Him I called to mind,
My blessings, family, peace of mind.

B Smith

CARING

Dear God, you send us love and hope
But we still forget to trust,
In Your kindness and Your caring
Though we really know we must,
Our cares and woes of mortal life
Fill us full of doubt,
But when we pause and ponder
You are all around us, all about.

You are in the eyes of children
The eyes of animal and bird,
And the music of the water
Has sounds we've not yet heard,
Make us stop and think of You
As each flower we peruse,
And see Your wondrous beauty
In things as yet unused.

Open our eyes and let us see
What things must really count,
Dispel our need for useless gain
We need just a small amount,
Let us put away things of pleasure
Have our minds on better things,
And when the time is ready,
May our souls have silver wings . . .

Margaret Beetham

HE IS RISEN

Yes 'tis April once again
Lambs skip free on the hills
Yes 'tis April once again
Daffodils bloom at will
Yes 'tis April once again
Good Friday draweth nigh
Thoughts turn to the Lamb of God
Nailed on a cross to die.

Sunday morn what a triumphant call
Christ is risen redemption for all.
Easter time another year
Lambs on hill tops call
Thoughts turn to the Lamb of God
Sacrifice for all.

Took our place
Our sins He bore
King of Kings
Crown of thorns He wore
Message remains the same
As that first Easter morn
When the Hallelujah
Cry went forth, He is risen

Man may live for evermore.

Frances Gibson

I WISH I WAS AT CALVARY

I see His blood in the rose that grows
I see His tears of sadness in every shower of rain
His love surrounds me everywhere I go
I wish I was at Calvary when my Saviour was in pain.

The pain He felt so long ago upon that cruel cross
Still hurts me deep inside even though I wasn't there
He shed His precious blood to free us from sin's power
It was a holy message to sinners everywhere.

Sometimes I hear His gentle voice as He calls to God above
And the tears run down my cheeks to wash His pain away
His eyes reveal a broken heart that my sin helped to break
I hope God will forgive me as upon my knees I pray.

Maurice Cardwell

A STILL, SMALL VOICE

Here, I hear no seagulls cry.
For deafened by the crush of foamy waves,
My ears are tuned to heed
A still, small voice.

Here, I see no man-made thing,
Nor strain my eyes to look beyond
Horizon's never-ending, omnipresent
Path to mystery.

Here, I sense a newness with each blast
Of icy gale, to blow the webs
Of city-woven mesh
From off my virgin soul.

Here, O living God
I feel Thy life and know Thy name.
Thy voice comes thundering
Softer, in a thousand-million ways.

But there my soul is silenced,
Starved and strained
'Midst those whose world of sound
Extends from ear to ear.

Sylvia Lester

LISTEN

Lord, help me be still,
>to simply adore you,
>to wait before you,
>and hear what you say.

Lord, help me listen carefully,
>help me listen prayerfully:
>Let me hear you speaking -
>Help me discern your way.

Lord, make me quick to listen -
>May I be slow to speak.
>I know your gifts are precious,
>But it's the *Giver* that *I* seek.

Lord, don't let me sit sleeping,
>At home with my folded hands here.
>May I be a *doer* of your Word
>and not just an *idle ear*.

Heather M Simpson

PEACE

Not even a bird breaks their silence
As they lie there so peaceful below
Though the leaves on the trees they do flutter
Not a sound do they make as they blow.
It's so quiet, I only hear heartbeats
Going faster than ever before
Beating right from the hearts of their loved ones
As they gently place flowers in a bowl.
Not a breath or even a teardrop
Can disturb them from sleep so divine
Such peace can only be granted
To us, when life's race is run
Peace be Thine, Peace by Mine, as we know it
Here on earth, as we both struggle on.

Margaret Rose Stewart

THOUGHTS ON A WINTER'S MORN

God there is a beauty in a winter's morn
That nature in its glory doth adorn;
The sky, the trees stately stand but not forlorn.

The birds long past their dawn chorus cry,
As they float on the wind, against the background of the sky.
How sweetly does the quiet peace tranquilly lie.
In earth and heaven, only thou canst know why.

Down the lane there's a rabbit's burrow;
He's not been out yet, perhaps he's sleeping now.
The neighbour's cat has been on the prowl
And, yes, the sheep and cows in the meadows low.

We would wish that all mankind might more often
    stop and stare -
Just to know that you are there.
Yes, Lord! Thank you for the dawn
That nature in its glory doth adorn.

Robin Edward Fisher

GOD'S DAY

When our days are slipping by.
And we're past the half-way flight
We look at life now, and we sigh
Sunrise o'er, sunset now, coming night.

Sunrise the youth of life and joy,
Where nothing only love is seen
Sunset next, thinking what was
    or could have been.
Night, when we reflect the passing
    years, and smile,
All has been glorious in
    God's lovely day.

Pauline A Taylor

BIND ME LORD

Lord bind my heart with your love,
That I will not forget you,
And set my mind on things above,
As you would have me do;

Lord bind my tongue with your word,
That I may speak with grace,
And allow your guidance to command,
My step in every place;

Lord bind my mind with understanding,
Fill me with joy and patience too,
So that some day when you return,
I will not feel ashamed before you!

Lord bind my hands with strength,
To *go the extra mile* at length;
That all work that I will do,
Will bring praise and honour back to you!

Esther Armstrong

THE HEDGEROW MESSAGE

Dear God I thank you for this lovely morn,
My footsteps hasten to that stretch of road,
Where all creation opens up its arms
And burdening cares no longer are my load.

For there my feet are borne on bluebird wings,
My heart explodes in wild and rapturous song,
Once more those crimson clumps of joy,
Reach out to touch me as I pass along

For many months this hedgerow now has bloomed,
To autumn's golden touch I saw it thrill,
'Though oft' times shrouded in the mist and rain,
It still delights my eye in winter's chill.

This hedgerow speaks of one who came to serve,
The Prince of Peace to whom wise men were led,
The thorns remind me of the crown He wore
The crimson berries of the blood He shed.

Unchanging as the beauty He creates,
His love for us will still come shining through
Look out my friend upon this Christmas time
The message in the hedgerow blooms for you.

Joan E Creighton

FOREVER TRUE

When the trails of life can get you down
Wear a smile never a frown
Keep a twinkle in your eye
Never moan or give a sigh
He is watching from on high.
Just be thankful for the life
The Lord hath given you
And always do remember
He is forever true
Now that's a promise to believe
So the Bible says
Read it lovingly each day
And you'll never go astray
When your path's not easy
Take it slowly then
Stop along the highway
Always make a friend
Count your many blessings
O'er and o'er again
Remember that there's sunshine
Even after rain
So do be guided by His love
And thank Him for His care
He knows each, and everyone of us
And does our sorrows share
Then make your way throughout this life
Your aim you can fulfil
You may fall, and rise again \
But that's the good Lord's will.

Chrissie Dunn

THE LINE TO HEAVEN

Keep the line to Heaven open
It's a busy line to God!
Talk to Him daily
Thank Him for his immeasurable love
Thank Him for each little blessing
He bestows upon life's way
Ask Him to show you now
How you can serve Him best today
Ask Him for inspiration
As you search His holy word
You'll be blessed more each day
As you're guided heavenward!

M Ferguson

UNTITLED

Love no other God
but me,
and I will
set you free.

Love thy neighbour
as thy self,
and pray to God
to give them health.

When on earth
do not kill,
because we know
it's against God's will

Obey your mum
and dad
or you will end up
sad

Let these words be a
message to you
if you obey them God will
love you through and through

A Baird

COUNTRY TIME

Dawn has come.
The darkness gives way to a dim blue light,
Contradicting the red feathery clouds that lay still over the hills
The fields lay still, asleep under a blanket of mist,
   broken in places by glens and hedges.
The ash and hazel that bear witness to many a sight smell or sound
    nurture a ewe with two new born.
But, as the lambs lay on fresh spring grass,
    the vixen turns to her mate in the den,
    gently embracing his musky coat.

Noon has come,
Robin, blackbird in song alike,
Are now joined by the chatter of tits, sparrows,
and the little wrens with the most powerful voices, to praise the new light.
A pair of legs stand rooted in the river as the oak would on sturdy ground
Their owner lies in wait,
watching a frog swim towards the silt covered bank,
Suddenly it meets its fate within the Heron's grasping bill,
its crest erect and fishy eyes still.

Evening has come.
Now the day has come of age.
The farmer collects both lamb and ewe.
He smells the vixen, her dense dark scent,
but she is safe in her hidden dwelling.
And so is the rabbit in his underground palace.
Before the shepherd has gathered his harvest,
the skies white matrix burst its banks of snow.
And so as the day ends with clear moon lit heavens,
the snow lies thick upon the earth.
Soon though with snowdrops at hand,
comes the spring, salvation to the land.

Luke Teacy (16)

PILGRIMAGE TO ISRAEL

We travelled to Jerusalem,
Where our pilgrimage began;
The hills and valleys all portrayed
A very arid land.

We climbed to Paternoster,
Mount of Olives then to view
The scenes of many great events
Of Jerusalem old and new.

Having crossed the Kidron valley,
Entered the Upper Room;
While there upon Mount Zion,
We saw King David's Tomb.

To Bethlehem we hastened
And viewed the Manger Square;
Where Jesus Christ was born for us
In a stable cold and bare.

We ascended to Massada,
Then down to the Dead Sea;
Soon on to Jericho's ancient walls
And the shores of Galilee.

We visited the Garden Tomb,
Where precious time was shared
With others as we sang and prayed
To God above who cared

For sinners just like me and you,
God sent His Son to save;
He bled and died and rose again,
Victorious o'er the grave.

Edwina Ritchie

BEFORE THE DAWN

From over the hills where tomorrow lies
A paler grey comes into the skies
And there through the trees
Where the moon gleam ebbs
Dew drops are bright on the spiders' webs

And under the hedgerow and through the hay
Small furry creatures prepare for the day
And high in the trees
Waits the morning thrush
Poised to end the brightening hush

Beyond the slopes where the sun will rise
Pink cotton blossom fingers the skies
And here 'neath the trees
In the quiet I pray
And thank my God for another day.

Claude H Bigg

YOUR LOVE

So much worry in our hearts,
But really we are not that far apart,
For I feel that you are always there for me.
Your love grows outward like a willow tree.
You always seem to forgive and forget
And for anytime I forgot you, I regret,
The times when my life took over my mind,
And to your love my heart was blind,
And then I remember you when I was in desperation
But when I called You, there was no hesitation,
You came and showed me the light,
Out of darkness into sight.
You are a God I can always turn to
No matter what I say and do
Even when I forget to repent my sin,
Your love for me still remain like an outer skin.
God, I must thank you for the things you give me each day,
For really I love you in every way.
I feel your love when nothing else seems right,
Never God may I feel that you are out of sight.

Sarah Walsh (14)

A PART TO PLAY

Oh what, Sadness with grief hard to bear.
Families now incomplete.
As we gaze, on that vacant chair.
God gives us strength the days to meet.

In a country torn apart.
Now so many with a broken heart.
The news, each day, so depressing.
For another family so distressing,

Oh what sorrow, filled us all.
We prayed to God a pleading call.
That peace would soon return again.
Dialogue take place by women and men.

Ordinary folk should have a say
Have a decent part to play.
How this country should be run.
Reconciliation having begun.

None too arrogant, none too proud.
Just be themselves, and clear the cloud.
To think of others should be their aim.
A desire to help the weak and lame.

Oh help us Lord, in this hour of need.
To sew the seed of loving seed.
Upon our hearts so warm, so true.
Others first is nothing new.

Enter the homes of our land, we pray.
Courtesy and consideration to be the rule of the day.
A kind deed shown, a helping hand.
Will create a happier land.

Elizabeth Swaile

PURE JOY!

God of my life,
Hear me when I pray
You are the one of wonders,
And of nature.

You made everything
I have seen,
You even made me.

I have joy in my heart,
That you are always there,
You are my friend,
And heavenly father.

Samantha Britton

JOY TO THE WORLD

Panting excitedly, squeals of delight,
Sweaty palms clench paper,
He's coming tonight!
Grab a pen - quick!
Scribble your desires,
Anything's possible in a couple of hours.
'Joy to the World', voices sing out,
Labyrinths of holly and tinsel about,
Rustling of paper and tape fills the ears
Trees creaking with items once thought too dear!
Human emotions rarely exposed
Behind a door that's constantly closed,
Ajar for once allowing goodwill
Expressed, if only, purchased at tills
'Look at the time! He'll not come tonight'
All off to bed without a fight
The glow from the fireside warms the heart
Empty boxes of chocolates signals the start.
Settle down to *the* movie 'Oh! No! Where's the tape?'
Panic sets in and alters the state
Disappointment? Oh! No! There is no danger,
And remember the child that lay in the manger. . .

Karin McBride

THE FINAL PARTING OF OUR WEDDING VOWS

Oh, my darling, when I am dead and gone
Please, do not weep over me too long.
For has not God let me love you all these years
So please, my sweetheart - dry your tears.
To me you have been a true and Godly wife
Loving and standing by me all my life
But now my life, it has past and gone
My love for you Audrey, with God's help will carry on
And if in death, Jesus Christ allows loving memories to stay
Then I will love you and meet beyond judgement day
And after Armageddon's been sighted
Then through God, Jesus Christ and Holy Ghost
We will be united.

So until that time does come to pass
Keep your pecker up - good lass.
Go on pick up your future life
Take hold of God's love and courage, you showed as my wife
To me you will always be my loving Audrey.

(Goodbye my love, my life, my lady)
Until we reach God's promised land.
Remember me as your ever loving husband.

Albert Shepherd

JESUS I'M YOURS

Jesus I offer my life to you,
Take me and shape me in all that I do,
Fill me with praise and fill me with love.
Be always present with your Grace from above.

If I should stumble or if I should fall,
Lift me my Saviour and carry me on,
In you I take refuge, with you at my side,
I will fear nothing, you'll be my guide.

'Come all to me' who are burdened down low,
And I will refresh you, wherever you go,
'Come you and take from the food that I give'
'Come follow me and then you shall live.'

'What more dear friends could our Saviour do?'
He died for me and he died for you,
Jesus I'm thirsty,
Let me drink from your spring,
Jesus you knock,
Please come on in.

Teresa Murray

A MORALITY POEM . . .

'Let not the sun go down upon your wrath,'
Help light to shine upon another's path.
If quarrels start, a peacemaker, you,
Will help to talk the problems through . . .

Ruth gleaned, among the alien corn,
Food left for those who were forlorn . . .
And so, may we, God's blessings share,
To help someone a load to bear . . .

'Do unto others, as you would
That they should do to you.'
Show that God's love from Heaven above
Shines all our lifetime through . . .

Winifred Richardson

THE GIFT OF SIGHT

What would life be like without the gift of sight,
Imprisoned in a world of permanent night?
Have you e'er stopped to ponder a theme such as this,
Grasping the immensity of all we would miss?
The delicate beauty of a flower, petals unfurled;
The many scenic wonders of our so diverse world -
Oceans pounding the coastline, a cascading waterfall,
The snow-capped summits of towering mountains so tall;
The scorching noon-day sun blazing down from the skies;
The inquisitiveness in a little child's eyes;
The radiant bride and proud husband, their bliss unconcealed,
Their heartfelt vows of love by a tender kiss sweetly sealed.
The myriad of colours could not thrill the heart,
Nor could we enjoy reading or viewing works of art.
Monuments to man's achievements could not inspire,
Even the opposite sex we could not admire.
Into our loved ones' faces we could not gaze at all,
Ne'er seeing their smiles, furrowed brows nor their teardrops fall.
Yes, our lives truly are enriched to a major degree
By everything all around we are privileged to see,
And considering these things it is surely only but right
That we thank the God of creation for the priceless gift of sight.

Ian Caughey

PRESENCE PROMISED

'My presence shall go with thee
And I will give you rest'
This promise God has given me
My spirit has been blest
He knew how much I needed Him
When I cast on Him my care
And in my lonely moments
I knew that He was there.

He's in the deepest valley
He's on the highest hill
And when I call upon Him
My need He will fulfil
He knows my deepest heartache
My sorrows and my tears
For He walks along beside me
To banish all my fears.

So leaning on His promises
I live from day to day
And talking to my Lord in prayer
I will not go astray
I tell him all my problems
When my soul is sore distressed
He said 'My present shall go with thee
And I will give you rest.'

Elaine Irwin

THE BIG CHURCH

Some Sundays I don't
Attend Church.
Instead, I sit in
God's great cathedral,
Built of trees and hedges,
Pews of mossy banks,
Steeples of pointed hills,
Congregated by
Insects, birds and animals.
Hymns are sung by
My feathered friends,
While the animals
Repeat the prayers.
Sense the greatness of creations,
Observe each specie in relation.
There is friendliness,
Love and compassion,
Even horror and despair,
As predators take to the air.
Hear the invisible preacher,
To those who wish to hear,
'God's spirit is everywhere.'

R Harkness

PEACE AND GRACE

Oh God sometimes I wonder where
You are when there is trouble in
The family or out far
In ages past all a
Man had to worry about
Was would he be hungry
Or to wear any clout
Now there's muggings
Murders and rape
No time to talk
But make money that's great
No time it seems
To chew the cud
With a friend
Or neighbour
Only one's own blood
Fill all people's hearts
With peace and grace
Make Ireland a warming
Welcoming place.

J D Devlin

MY LITTLE CANDLE

I have a little candle
And I keep it burning bright
For I want to shine for Jesus
In the darkest night.

To keep my candle burning bright
To Sunday school I go
And there I hear of Jesus
And how He loves me so.

I must be very careful
That no sin I go about
For if I slide or stumble
My candle may go out.

Lily Stewart

THE TREE

From humble beginning close to the ground
A struggling young seeding there can be found
As it makes its way upwards year after year,
It grows taller and taller without any fear.

As it stretches its branches and raises its head
The birds of the air in its bosom are bred,
But then one day to no avail,
Men did come that tree to fell.

Not for some work of art,
Or something splendid set apart,
But was hewn down to bear a curse
Upon the Son of God who died for us.

Then carried along a bumpy road.
On a shredless back was borne this load.
Too much it was for that Man of Grace
Another was made to take His place.

Then to a hill it was traced
And upon it was the Saviour placed
With not a murmur or a cry
Jesus was lifted up there to die.

Then when the world had done its worst,
Jesus cried with a loud burst.
It is finished was what He said.
As the price for sin was fully paid.

Now to all who look upon that cross.
To the One who died for all the lost.
Full redemption can it be
From the One who died upon that tree.

Thomas Patterson

REJECTED AND DESPISED?

That morn at half past six the voice came through
On the telephone - 'I thought you ought to know that Hugh
       Poor Hugh', (after endless months of pain), 'is dying.'

At 7am the priest with book came by and read and prayed
That God, if he so willed, would see death's hand delayed.
       Hugh's wife, not yet prepared for parting, stood by crying.

At seven fifteen the doctor made a short inspection,
Shrugged gestures of despair, gave Hugh a strong injection.
       'Not much chance but it's at least worth trying.'

At noon poor Hugh was fast asleep - they deemed it 'In a coma.'
The sympathetic neighbours came and savouring death's aroma,
       Hastily departed, soulfully sighing.

At 6pm Hugh moaned and opened wide his eyes,
The watchers at his bedside stifled flabbergasted cries,
       Hugh was bent, it seemed, once more on death defying.

In the subsequent debate the reasons for his non-demise
Were weighed, assessed and all agreed, 'Surprise -
       Of that there's simply no denying!'

But God and prayer, the doctor's skill, and even the injection
Were each in turn considered and each labelled with rejection.
       'Fighter Hugh,' it was declared. 'had strengths beyond espying.'

Sidney McCullough

FAITH

Oh Lord, help me!
I don't know what's going on!
Ahhh!
Yes . . . No . . . Well, maybe.
I thought, think, thought I believed.
Why? . . . Why? . . .
Maybe I still do . . .
I just don't know, I can't be sure.
 . . . Give me a sign?
Help me if You're there,
Am I wasting my time?

Is there a 'Big Guy in the Sky?'
I am starting to doubt.
Have I lost my faith?
Or was it all an illusion?

Has the 'polished being' become tarnished?
Or is it just that,
I can't see God any more?
I feel no love for things I don't see.
I don't know if I ever did.

What is religion?
What is God?
An illusion?
Your mind playing tricks?
Maybe we do just live then die.

Abigail Durrans

ALL

All those many years ago a rugged cross stood high,
And upon that cross there hung our Saviour Lord, to die,
His love filled life, did not deserve to be by man cut short,
But as 'twas written, so it was, our souls His dear blood bought,

All man's sins and for all time, that blood has washed away,
'Twill never lose its cleaning power, to wash the meanest clay,
The many years of sacrificing, that day at last was done,
The ultimate sacrifice of all - the dying of God's Son!

All those who've heard the story of how He rose again
In Glory and in Power, defeating death and pain,
Should pause and ponder deeply, and search their hearts anew,
And draw oh, ever closer, to our precious Lord, so true.

All is what dear Jesus wants, all we should freely give,
All is what He gave for us, to show how we should live.
All the many souls today, that have not heard His name,
Must be told of Salvation free, it's here, since Jesus came!

Alice Eileen Coates

A PRAYER

Lord help me daily to bear my cross
What e're that cross may be
For Thou dost know in gain or loss
Just what is best for me

Lord give me grace to follow Thee
Wherever Thou dost lead
Though knowest the path that's best for me
Lord, You know just what I need

When I am tempted to go astray
And do what I should not do
Give me the needed strength I pray
To cast my all on You.

R B McKenzie

THE TWILIGHT BIRD

The bird sings cheerfully the song
Flooding twilight the night not long
As its white has turned so dull
Evening creeps upon a lull

Over there the moon has shed
Source in the water which finally lead
So little bird make your last catch
Calling for home it's leafy lay batch

The trees home strong and secure
Even storm it will surely endure
Let the broadened leaves make you so snug
With eyes at rest take the last cud.

J P Sutton

QUESTIONS AND ANSWERS

What is the thing to look for
And from where did it come said he
Why look for it anyway
And how does it matter to me
I'll tell you the answer because
It's the way of the world you see
To search for wisdom and knowledge
For by trying and testing's the key
One searched for ever and ever
And then at the end of the day
When one examines his lifestyle
He will find that it was not the way
The way of the cross is by far the best
And it doesn't take questions to find
If you stop for a moment to consider
That Jesus is the answer to questions
Of a far more worthier kind.

S G Thompson

A MEDITATION OF LIFE

The thorns of life, may cause you pain,
You wonder, does anyone really understand.
If you look to Jesus, He has the answer,
Right in the palm of His hand.

He will lead you through the darkness,
His glory will light your way
His love will guide and protect you
Bringing you into the brilliant light of day.

Jesus does understand
Every step of life that we take
Loneliness, sorrow, rejection
He went through these for your sake.

When we walk through the door of suffering
And we feel the burden too much to bear.
Call upon the Lord in prayer
You will find the answers there.

Open your eyes to the One,
Who lived by His Father's will
He died, rose again and ascended
And He reigns now in Heaven still.

Judith Cooper

NATURE'S WONDER

Just as a child I stand and gaze
O'er landscape clothed in golden blaze,
I wonder what almighty power
Has made this earth in such grandeur?

Rabbits go hippity-hop down their burrows
Tiny Willy-Wagtails scoop round the furrows
Sparrows busily lining their nest
With moss and feathers and all of the best.

The old grey mare surveys her foal
With loving eyes and secrets untold.
And Daisy, the cow - oh so lazily lies
Whilst her calf, it over the meadow glides.

How did God create these beings so fine
Will still remain a mystery of mine -
As I eagerly watch the changes of season
I ponder . . . and ponder . . . but can't give a reason.

Heather Patterson

WORDS OF COMFORT

Lord Jesus Thou art here to Comfort Help and Cheer,
No other friend can come so near, to soothe away our fear.
Thou givest strength for each new day, and help in time of need,
And by the sweetness of Thy Presence proves Thyself a friend indeed.
Lord Jesus keep me Trusting and Cleaving unto thee,
While life shall last, and all trials past - and Thy Blessed Face I see.
For then it will be Joy to look upon Thy Face,
And dwell with Thee for evermore saved by Thy Wonderful Grace.

Ethel Wright

THANKSGIVING

We thank you Dear Lord for the break of day
We thank you for listening to us while we pray
We thank you for comfort in our hour of need
For your reassurance us your flock you doth lead.

We thank you for sending your own Precious Son
To die on the Cross and free us from sin
To all who believe on him - Salvation is free
God's wondrous gift - to sinners like me

We thank you for loved ones, now gone from our midst
Who turned to the Saviour and accepted his gift
We pray for all people, who are still in their sins
And trust in the Saviour, these souls He will win

We thank you Dear Lord, for your promise
That you our Saviour - will soon return again
To take all your people home to Glory
To dwell with you, for ever and ever Amen:

Amy Gordon

HOPE

The days are getting longer,
Christmas will soon be here,
I'm really glad it's Friday
Or, our holiday is so near.

I'm glad today is over
Things can only improve
If this house no longer suits us,
We can always move.

Tomorrow can only get better
It can't be as bad as today.
Look, the rain is disappearing
Sunshine is on its way.

Someday, maybe, hopefully
Without it where would we be
This hope which keeps us going
Another day to see.

Remember, though when hoping,
Tomorrow is not ours,
The present is all we're sure of,
Not even the next few hours.

No doubt we'll keep on hoping
A better day to see
But in our thoughts we must include
God willing or DV

Joan Williamson

UNTITLED

No college in this land of ours
taught God his skills and special powers
to paint a sunset red and blue
a splendour for us all to view.

Or build a mountain of rocks and stone
A special skill all of His own
to reach the clouds and far above
And even touch us with His love.

He's not just an artist with brush and pen
A graphic designer ideas no end
The frost can glisten as I stand and listen
And as I'm debating, He's still creating.

The marvels the wonders the great and the small
I challenge the best one to fathom it all
I look at the beauty and what can I say
Was it all made from nothing at the start of life's day.

I don't need reminding that God made it all
The birds and the trees the wind and the leaves
I cherish the moment as I look at the sea
And wonder why gravity won't set it free.

A master designer of whom I am proud
To be part of his company away from the crowd
Where in the quietness I ponder and wonder
Why He made me in his image to see.

Leslie Clyde

ON RETREAT

Lord, help me
why am I here?
I am seeking Your face
yet I am afraid to look.
Afraid of what I may see in myself
when the darkness lifts.

Why am I afraid of You?
As Adam and Eve in the garden
I want to hide myself.
Let me be like a child
innocent and unashamed,
standing before You, unafraid
Lift me into Your light, Lord
heal my heart
set me free.

The darkness seems safe,
yet I am deceived.
In the dark there is danger,
suffocation.
The breath of my prayer
grows ever weaker
as I smother in this night.
Without your light I will die.

Lord, help me
I am seeking your face.
Bathe me in Your light
Show me myself as I am
Pure and holy, cleansed by Your Love.
Give me a vision for what I can be -
Christ living in me.

Yvette Fulton

REMEMBRANCE

Death came as a friend,
quietly, compassionately, peacefully,
refusing to watch anymore, or stay its hand
and a soul gushed forth across the land,
as a flash of light, before God's sight,
an innocent life at an end.

I remember a humble figure answering the mass bells' call,
with a dignified faith, a true child of Saul.
Not for her the shining of light before men,
but rather, the profession of a quiet witness
and then, stealing away unobtrusively out of sight.
Such were the gentle ways, that marked each and all her
days, enshrining them forever.

She went from our midst, so quietly and softly,
her spirit moving through the day,
leaving us in abject sorrow
to face a numb and shocked tomorrow.
Truly her life was bright and clean,
a shining star, a radiant gleam,
from its inception to its end.

Weep not then, rather, take heart. This I know.
She is with God.

M J Murray

THE LIGHT FROM ABOVE

The Light from above
Shone down with love
On me
On me.

He came from above
And gave His love
To me
To me.

He taught me to love
My sisters and brothers,
He
Taught me.

Now I'll teach His word
'Til all have heard
From me
From me.

No more need to search
So come to His Church
With me
With me.

Jacqueline Maguire

GOD IS SO GOOD

God is so good
He gave us clothes to wear
He gave us food
That's more than fair

He loves us all
black or white
large or small
despite or plight

God wants us all to come home
That he's made very clear
He does not want us to come alone
But with the Holy Spirit ever near.

Jill Warrington (13)

GOD

We only have one God
Patient, kind and true
No other person in all the world
Will be as true to you.
He is so kind
He is so good
He will always trust in you
As long as you trust in him.
He gives us health
He gives us ourselves
He gave us nature as well

Christine Montgomery (11)

A SPECIAL FRIEND

God is a Saviour to me,
He died on a cross for me,
When I was lost He saved me,
And now He is a special Friend to me.

God is a special Friend to me,
He helps me and looks after me,
When I am weak He strengthens me,
When I am sad He makes me glad.

Lyndsey McDougall (12)

BIG BROWN EYES - LOVE ME!

Last night Dundonald was filled
With Christians and non alike,
Enjoying a gospel evening together
With Cliff - an inspiration alright.

Rocks and Gospel together
We swayed to and fro with delight
A message of our Saviour's blessings
We surely can count them tonight.

'Saviour's Day' and others we heard.
Bill Latham and Cliff in discussion.
But the most poignant moment for me was
Those beautiful Big Brown Eyes.

A little boy begging for mercy
'Please give me some love and affection'.
Then ever so slowly the sadness
Turned into a broad grin of gladness.

Just one moment was captured on film
Of one little boy's Big Brown Eyes
But those eyes spoke more to me personally,
Of God's Love and His Son's Sacrifice.

So finally - if only one person
Tonight feels a stirring within.
A lifetime of Love from Our Saviour
Is surely the reward from our sins.

Geraldine Campbell

THE GREATEST DAY

In Bethlehem long long ago
A baby boy was born,
Jesus was the baby's name
On that first Christmas morn.

It's celebrated ever since
By people black and white.
It is a very happy time
And everyone's delight.

Carol singers in the street
Bring joy to every door,
Their singing asks for peace on earth
No-one could wish for more.

Little children wait for Santa
Great suspense as dawn draws near
Eyes do pop and eyes do sparkle
When all the toys they want are here.

Presents cards nice things to eat
Are on show that day,
And decorations all around
Make everything so gay.

Church bells ringing snowflakes falling
It's a great and glorious scene
Snowmen mistletoe and holly
The greatest day that's ever been

T Alexander

NATURE

Everything in the world is so beautiful,
The flowers, the animals, and the trees
God made everything which is so wonderful,
From all the animals to the bees.

The beautiful green trees and the lovely blue sky.
The cute little animals and the sun and the moon,
It would be awful if we were to die.
And the time that the birds start singing is noon.

Charlene Brown (12)

WHY ME?

Why Me Lord? Why me?
Who was I but a lost sinner
Plodding along by the ways of this world
But there you saw me, a mere speck in society
To you I was worth saving.

Did I not close you out 'til now?
Did I not deny your importance for life?
To be without you is to be without hope
Not hope alone for the doors are thrown open
And your spirit overflows.

You lift me up and enwrap me with love
That hardness softens and rivers flow
Forgive my sinful being and let the spirit of Christ
fill my veins
Praises be to God, for He did not forsake me.
I thank thee for answering my cry.

Why me Lord? Why not me?!

Cherie Hunter

A LAST FAREWELL

Goodbye, my dear old friends,
with your, sanctifying strains.
Now time, has caught up on me,
life's end nears, to kill my pains.

Anointed, with your tears,
I do long, for dying breath.
A choir, of singing Angels,
soothe me to sleep, as I am blessed.

A beam, of piercing light,
splinters cloud, and spreads them thin,
Their gentle, cleansing raindrops,
then absolve, mere-mortal sin.

Gracious arms, now open,
reaching down, through clearing skies,
as I fall, to true temptation,
and rise-up high, above your cries.

Chris O'Hare

BE THANKFUL

When you look at folk in wheelchairs,
Who can't run and jump as you do,
Do you ever thank God for His goodness,
And the health and strength given to you.

Many today live in darkness,
Who have never seen a flower or a tree,
Depending on a guide dog to lead them,
Oh! do you thank God you can see.

There are those who can't hear or speak,
Never heard the birds chirp or sing,
A hearty laugh or the tick of a clock,
To them does not mean anything.

Millions today are hungry,
No choice of menu for their tea,
Maybe a slice of bread or a bowl of rice,
They're not over-weight you'll agree.

In cardboard boxes many sleep rough,
While many on mountains do roam,
Through poverty or war their homes had to flee,
Be thankful to God for your home.

Be thankful if you are enjoying good health,
Many ill and infirm in hospitals lie,
Give thanks to the Lord for all of His care,
For our needs He does richly supply.

Do pray for all who are in need of care,
Those handicapped in any way,
For the homeless, hungry or the ill,
We should not forget to pray.

Olive Williamsons

THE BOEHEMIAN

To the people who live
By the beat of a different drum.
To those who know the war is won
Before the battle's begun.
To the ones who have dropped
This life's humdrum affair,
Standing firm in belief
While the world strips them bare.
To each soul who goes public
With Christ as their king,
To each voice that's condemned
Every time that they sing.
To each hand reaching out
To a tormented world,
And whose heart keeps forgiving
As insults are hurled.
To the ones who stand tall
When the enemy tramples,
To those who have little
Yet know that it's ample.
To those putting self
Last before others.
The ones who stand up
For less fortunate brothers.
To those who offer an encouraging word,
For the ones praying earnestly to the Lord.
To all who believe
Against all the odds,
These are the ones
Who are most blessed by God.

Julie McLaughlin

JUST THINK

Just think, some night the stars will gleam
upon a cold grey stone
And trace a name with silver beam
And lo! 'twill be your own.

The time is speeding on to greet
Your epitaphic rhyme
Your life is but a little beat
Within the heart of time.

A little gain, a little pain,
A laugh and perhaps a moan
A little blame, a little fame
Then just a star-gleam on a stone.

W J Hughes

CARE OF THE AGED

When eyes grow dim and weak of limb
And frowns a smile erase -
When steps are slow, and back bent low,
It's the time we call old age.

Lest we forget, there's life there yet
The human heart a-beating.
A woman or man, who's lived life's span
And knows that time is fleeting.

On lonely nights by dim firelight
Tis many a tear does fall.
With no-one there, a trouble to share
If only we would call.

So we must give, each day they live
A reason for their living,
To let them know, we love them so,
Does not cost much in giving.

The days they spend, towards journey's end
Are in the years, they borrow.
Today we'll care, while they're still there,
Let's not wait until tomorrow.

Mary Josephine Devlin

PEACE

As we look around our land today,
Its beauty reigns supreme,
It's so hard . . . to imagine
All the suffering there's been.

The ceasefire now has come at last
And peace reigns once again,
But hearts are crushed with sorrow,
For the ones, who died in vain.

Someday we'll leave this scene of time,
To stand before God's throne,
We'll give account of all our deeds,
Each one will stand alone.

We'll wish that we could start again,
As we stand, hearts filled with sin,
We'll think of all the deeds we've done,
But, we'll find no peace within.

To the victims of the violence,
Our prayer for them should be,
That God will heal their broken hearts,
From the past He'll set them free.

Our Father up in Heaven
He too . . . suffered loss,
When He sacrificed His only Son,
To die upon a cross.

As He hung upon that cross
A murderer by His side,
Pleaded there for mercy.
Jesus answered . . . then He died.

Shirley Snowden

SHE HAD ALWAYS SEEMED UNDULY CASUAL

Contorted faces
In a shower of tears,
A barrage of wind
Resounds in their ears.

A fallen figurine
Too delicate to save,
Is raised to the heavens
And borne to the grave.

But what of her soul!
Did she earn salvation?
Will she rest in the peace
Of His new creation?

A handful of mourners
(Weighed down with prostration),
Strain for some strength
In the Reverend's oration.

Yet whatever they have
Or have not got,
Some may be strengthened
While others may not.

And as life still continues
And homewards they go,
Have they changed their perspectives?
The Lord only knows.

Paul Hutton

NEAR TO GOD

As I strolled through my garden this morning
I looked on such beauty so rare
The flowers of all different colours and shapes
I thought to myself oh, what can comapre

I looked at the tiny rose buds
In colours pink and white
To see my Saviour's handiwork
So beautiful perfect and right.

I see the little pansies and yes there's daisies too
Then there's the tulips and coloured sweet pea.
To smell that sweet aroma
As my eyes take in the view.

It's then I remember God's precious word
Which speaks of the lily so fair
How that King Solomon in all his splendour
With this flower could not be compared.

K E Climond

SOMETHING INSIDE ME . . .

Something inside me tells me these things
As sure as a bird has feathery wings
When to laugh and when to scorn
When to be happy, and when forlorn.

Something inside me tells me these things
When to be quiet, when to have flings
When to push forward head high and proud
Or when to be an ordinary chap in a crowd.

Something inside me tells me these things
The feeling of joy that real good luck brings
The wellbeing and warmth that comes from the sun
The feeling of assurance when having great fun.

Something inside me tells me these things
The real meaning of words like 'arrows' and 'slings'
The quality of air can vary each day
As can the quality of man in every way.

Something inside me tells me these things
Such as the absolute pain just when a bee stings
The beautiful sound of a peal of church bells
Is as different to me as a football crowd's yells

Somethings inside me tells me these things
The differing sound 'tween woodwind and strings
But the greatest thing this something can tell
Is the considerable difference 'tween heaven and hell.

Paul Harvey Jackson

LAMBING TIME

The Shepherd shelters in a shady nook
He's a twinge in the back so he leans on his crook
When lambs are a coming the rain does the same
He often says it's the Lord's wee game.

He thinks to himself he'll surely get to Heaven
For it's way past midnight and he was up before seven.
The lambs are too big and he's prone to curse
For there's two under his coat that he has to nurse.

The cold and the wet will quite a few kill
And the fox licks his lips for he's had his fill
But the Shepherd looks aloft with a twinkle in his eye
For he knows full well who's up on high.

He knows that soon it will all settle down
And the lambs will then be frolicking around
He whistles a hymn and in prayerful mood
Thanks his Lord above for all that is good.

Drew Robinson

JUST ONE TOUCH

She was desperate and had a great need.
For many years her pennies she did spend.
Every doctor far and near knew her by name
None of them could cure her they were all the same.

The situation was getting worse, never better,
The pain so severe, it was hard to bear.
One day she heard Jesus was coming to town
Surely He could help, He had such renown.

She left early one morning not to miss out
She wanted to see Him, she didn't want to shout,
There He was standing just in front of her eyes
She waited a while, there were so many cries.

At last she picked up courage and reached out
Her faith so great she didn't have to shout
She knew just one simple touch would do,
To heal her from her illness and every foe.

Yes, just one simple touch of His hem,
That was all, He did not condemn,
Her faith had made her whole again
She went on her way rejoicing with no more pain.

He can still touch us today on earth,
His healing power the same, there is no dearth,
Reach out and touch Him today
And you too will know His blessing always.

Irene Campbell

CALVARY

I sometimes think upon the Christ of God.
The only One who ever trod
The earth
And never sinned.
Yet even so by hands and feet
They pinned Him to a cross,
And fired on Him their ribald shafts of mirth.

And then I have to ask why was it so?
That mortal man could sink so low
To maim
And kill the Prince of Peace
And will the wonders of it ever cease
That One so pure,
Should be the butt of that dark day of shame.

R Johnston

\

DENY THE DOVE

The grass lay stained
by Saviour's grace
Through love alone
blood-stained His face

Love fought on
where flesh was torn
Love gave strength
through jeers and scorn

Stranger faces
but He knew them all
Each heart was His
as He answered the call

Crowds of hate
for the Man of Love
Frightened friends
deny the dove

He loved them still
for what was said
For you, for all
He lived and bled

Broken bones
gave way to steel
Wounds that bled
so we could heal

Was fear of truth
what killed the dove
Or simply Lord
you died for love?

Colin Arthurs

LOVE ONE ANOTHER

Throughout this Land
Walk hand in hand
Show love and kindness
To all that mind us.

No matter what
their colour or creed,
We'll show love
To all in need.

In good times and in bad
and to anyone who's sad,
We'll all sing together
and be happy in one land.

Mary Morgan

FAMINE

Purple Blossom, White Blossom
Long, long ago.
Acres of potatoes growing
In the fields round Ballinasloe.

Purple Blossom, White Blossom
Where did they go?
Acres of potatoes rotting
In the fields round Ballinasloe.

Purple Blossom, White Blossom
See how they grow
Lilac and Honeysuckle
O'er the graves round Ballinasloe.

Purple Blossom, White Blossom
Crops still fail, people die.
Dear Lord of Heaven
Why? Why? Why?

Victim of the Cross
Mighty Ruler of Men
Why is famine happening
Again and again?

Black Men, Brown Men,
Yellow and White Men too
In anguish call for help
To their Father, to You.

Please God, Where are you?

Catherine Brady

I'M A GRANNY NOW

It seems like only yesterday
I skated in the park,
and played beneath the gas-lamp,
when Belfast streets were dark
Dear God, you have been good to me,
A husband, kids, a home.
And now I start to wonder
Where all the years have flown . . .
I'm a Granny now!

I learned, and played, in childhood days
In the streets of North Belfast.
Then worked and danced my teens away,
Watched films from the past.
Dear God, three daughters fair you sent,
When I'd wed my husband true
You helped us bring them through their lives
As parents ought to do . . .
I'm a Granny now!

Time passed and two of them were wed,
Then soon each home had three.
Our eldest daughters started
to compile a family tree.
They each produced another child
Our joy was quite complete.
All heading for their teen-years now
The passing years so fleet . . .
I'm a Granny now!

Renee McAllister

MOTHER

In memory of my Mother,
I write these lines of verse;
Thinking of her love for me,
Wishing we could converse:

'So many years have passed, Mum,
Since God called you away;
I love you very much Mum,
Are the words I'd like to say.

But God loved you too, Mum,
So much He gave His Son;
To die on Calvary's Cross, Mum,
And prepare for you a home.

I know that one day too, Mum,
We'll both meet up above;
To be together again, Mum,
And enjoy God's perfect love.

Until that day is come, Mum,
In my thoughts you'll be;
As I travel on life's journey, Mum,
With memories of thee.'

James G Mercer

RHYME AND REASON

I know I believe there's a God above
Watching the things that go on.
I know I believe He offers His love
To those alive in His Son.
I'm sure that He's there
When I whisper a prayer
And ask Him to make Himself known.
I know that I hurt Him, demean Him, repel Him,
Expect Him to be the abused.
I play on my weakness and call on His grace,
Content to be the excused.

Alison McVea

PERFECT LOVE

No more doubts and no more fears,
No more walking back through the years
Jesus Christ is here to stay
He will guide me all the way.
He is the way, the truth, the light
No more darkness, no more night . . .
He is the bright and shining star
He is the essence of all we are
No more doubts and no more fears
Perfect love has healed all the years.

No more pain and no more tears
No more guilt of former years
The blood of Jesus covers all
He calls softly - my child walk tall -
He is Lord and He gives life
He takes away all hurt and strife
He is worthy to be praised
So bless the Lord, all your days.
No more doubts and no more fears
Perfect love has healed all the years.

Margaret Purdy

THE INDESCRIBABLE

How can you describe the indescribable -
Put a name to the Presence of the Lord?
How can you explain the inexplicable -
Not by picture, not by song, not by word.

There are just no words to describe Him,
All His glory, all His power, all His joy.
No explanation could ever explain Him,
We can only receive and enjoy.

If I sang a song for eternity,
Used an angel's tongue for my song,
Even then I could never express
All the praise that to Jesus should belong.

Yet, though these words are inadequate,
My lips unclean to even call Him Lord,
I will tell of His grace and mighty love,
And proclaim the beauty of His word.

Gloria Kearney

MAKE BELIEVE?

Without Jesus, where would we be?
We're living in a world of make-believe
Far from truth and full of pride
Sin is the game and the Truths denied.

Jesus said 'I am the Way, the Truth and the Life;
Abide in me by day and by night
For you I died at Calvary
I took your sins to set you free.

You must take the message now,
To all the world proclaim
Jesus Christ the Living Lord
Is going to come again.

Tell of my love and my nail-pierced hands
The blood I spread upon the ground
The miracles I did back then -
I'll do them now, in the face of men.

> You will believe in Me
> *I am* - The Son of God.

My spirit will flow over the nations
My spirit will set my people free
Spread the word, - declare salvation
You have the authority in Me.

Fiona Heath

IS ANYONE OUT THERE?

Under developed yet I am, my little heart is full of joy.
Huddled in a shallow shape, I feel secure in familiar surroundings.
Each beat of the heart comforts me, and the sense of excitement
provokes me to kick!

Ouch! - my tender body hurts.
I become soft and fail.
My under developed and delicate bodily functions weaken.
I am   . . dissolving!
What is happening? I am confused.

When I now look back from the heavens above at the life that
never was, saintly that I am, I still resent my mother's feeble actions.

Shauna Harley

UNTITLED

A moment's peace within a hectic life.
The silence of a minute or the stillness of the night.
A picture in the flames, your thoughts are set aside
And in God's peace abide.

Your fears are torn from wall to wall
And dreams are built on ground where doubts did fall.
And let your visions climb to homeward skies,
And in God's love abide.

Hear the noise within a silent prayer,
As God and Son speak loud and clear
'Be still and know that I am Lord
And God of all.'

Like stone, be still.
And take His love to you be fat and filled,
And close your eyes and listen,
Until your heart is still.

Joyce Ferguson

WHEN?

How?
How did this happen?
He came and told us a simple way
He came and showed us
How to please
Him.

Well?
What did we do?
We took what we wanted, and added to it.
We didn't want *His* easy way and
We still ask
Why?

Why
He allows sorrow?
Why *He* doesn't come again and take us
Haven't we learned anything?
We are the ones who have ignored
Him.

Ken Kissick

TURN TO HIM

When trouble's ahead, you know you can't face,
When good goes to bad and slowly gets worse,
When friends have all gone and you're lonely and scared,
When there's no-one to care, be there, understand.

He holds out His hands wounded and torn,
With tears in His eyes at the pain you have borne,
He's begging and pleading that you'll give it to Him
And He'll carry and bear it if you'll just turn to Him.

When you're carrying pain you can no longer bear,
If it's suddenly begun to consume all your care,
If you'll give Him your trust, in your burden He'll share.
For you'll never carry more than He and you can bear.

He stretches His arms to you open wide,
With nails in His hands and scar in His side,
No words does He utter, the pain's in His eyes,
The love and the want He cannot disguise.
That problem, that worry, that fear or that dread,
Just give it to Jesus for He'll always be there.

Kerry Whyte

THE PASSING

His passing was as quiet as a gently falling leaf
No pleas for an extension
No plans for future well being
No sad farewells;
A quiet gentle man in life
A quiet gentle man in death;
No dignitaries crowd the funeral Mass
No grand orations, no eulogies
Nor do Ministers in priestly garb adorn the altar;
One lone celebrant offers the Sacrifice.
A quiet gentle man in life
A quiet gentle man in death.

M T Breslin

HIDE AND SEEK

Oh God! Where are you? Where?
I sometimes say you play at hide and seek,
Are everywhere and nowhere to be found,
Evoking search from lure of flowers' bright hues,
Or silvery iridescent fishes' scales,
Or fountain blasts of summons from great whales.
Through the green depths of tumbling waves you stare
At me, and dare, but then collapse in foam,
Or peer from out the folds of wavering faith -
A presence felt,
Still bidding me to find, and seek and seek,
But at times I long for something more concrete
To lay my cheek against, and feel at rest,
And greet.

Joan-Pamela Moore

A DREAM

Last night I had a dream,
I dreamt I spoke to Jesus the Nazarene,
I felt so unworthy as I bowed my head in shame,
I said, 'Thou art my Lord, the Holy One
Praise be Thy Name.'

Amidst my fear and trembling, I did humbly ask,
'Father please help us, terrible things have come to pass,
We have murder and starvation, hate, greed and strife,
Men feel no remorse Lord,
When they take another's life.

I feel so afraid, for children yet unborn
For all mankind upon the earth, the fear about the bomb,
The money that is spent on rocket-ships for space
While a little child is starving,
Tears wet upon his face.'

He looked at me in compassion and slowly he did say
'Be not afraid my child it was so in my day,
Man will not listen, many disobey
Two paths I have given him
He must choose the way.'

'But what is, and what is to come, must be,
Yet all men can be saved if they will only follow me
Fear not now I say to you, watch always and pray,
Peace will come unto the earth
On my appointed day.'

M Johnston

WHICH DO YOU PREFER?

Guys, which do you prefer?
Beautiful young girls with their long blond hair?
Or which fella in a crowd would stand out?
The type that all the girls go crazy about.
Tall, dark and handsome, small blond and sweet
This is the type of fella we would all love to meet
It's in human nature to go for the good looks.
A cute smile here and there was all that it took.

OK, maybe you prefer those who make you laugh and are fun,
'You're young, free and single, life has just begun,
So let's not lose sleep over a night out here and there,
But listen young Christian, you must beware!
Who is to know? A relationship might form,
Stuck in a situation, reform or conform.
God is too precious to let slip away
Take caution in love, as trials could easily come your way.

So now my friend which do you prefer?
To attract someone to you, is that really fair?
To lure them by your looks and charm,
Unknowingly, you could be doing someone harm,
You may fall in love and never want to part,
Haven't you heard, God looks at the heart?
Which is more appealing, to be loved by someone who is lost?
Or, only loved by Jesus whose life was your cost?

No, I'm not suggesting that your life be a bore,
But other's feelings and emotions you just can't ignore
'You can be in the world but not of it'
Young Christian where does your heart sit?

The world and God are like oil and water they cannot combine,
Get your priority right, do you really mean, Your will, not mine?

Olivia E J Clarke

CREATION V EVOLUTION

What's your opinion today my friend'
On the theories of so-called intelligent men
When they say that the earth and the skies and the seas
Is the gelling together of the *big bang* debris.

It's a theory of man led by Satan's delusion
To frustrate even more the mind in confusion
To deny the foundation of all we believe
The account of the bible they say is naive

What God brought about on the space of six days
Took millions of years this new theory says
And the man God created to share in His glory
Was one time a monkey, well that is their story

They say all their theories are backed up by science
But really it's only an act of defiance
Against a creator who makes great demands
That don't coincide with man's sinful plans

The falling of Adam and salvation's plan
In the book of creation was shown to man
To attack that creation is a real master stroke
For the whole building falls when the foundation's broke

So beware all you parents what your children are taught
Is it all based on scripture, if it's not then it ought
The whole trend today is to lead them astray
From the God of the bible and the straight narrow way

William Livingstone

FROM SHADOW TO SUBSTANCE

I dwell upon a part of earth green and fair
'Neath a great canopy, a changing sky,
In pain and pleasure of mortals to share
Seventy years, then this early part shall die.

Human love and hatred both our lot
Shared fellowship, bitter separation
Of these things who has tasted not?
Deep sorrow and Joy's pure elation.

But I pierce through this wide creation
To a three-fold Being greater far
Than any creature, however grand his station
To One beyond the light of sun or star.

Dare I who am a sinful child of earth
Claim audience with the Creator: Most High God
Who is a Spirit, I need a spiritual birth
Born of Spirit water and of blood.

Into His Presence none else may come
But those who come His way, *The Living Way*
Heirs of God through Christ, Heaven their home
The Spirit of God dwelling in them day by day.

God's Son stooped to die for my Redemption
God's spirit seeks to dwell and work in me
Oh wondrous love, beyond all comprehension
Boundless love, divine beyond degree.

Maureen Hawthorne

CALL ON ME

When your burden is heavy, and your body is weak,
for a respite from your pain, let I be the One you seek

When your heart is full of anguish
you've been dealt bitter blows
Call on Me for the answers, I am the one who knows

When night time falls and you are feeling all alone
fear not, I am there you don't have to be on your own

I ask for nothing from you only to be your friend, just
speak to Me sometimes and think of Me now and then

Your troubles will get easier your burdens will grow light
you shall emerge from the darkness and come into the light

All this I promise you if you can only see, I am always with you
My name is Jesus, please *call on me* . . .

Joseph Doherty

CALVARY

Blood flows freely from the crucified
Crimson coloured wine flows down
To a thirsty world,
From a gaping gash
The fresh, flesh-cut
In the Saviour's side.

Water-mingled blood flows soothingly,
Drenching the sinner's soul
Bathing him in Bethesda's pool,
Penetrating through the hardened skin
Dripping through pores to the heart within,
Melting mortal misery and the shame,
Dissolving dirt,
A sanctifying rain,
Giving joy where sadness once was rife,
Instead of death, a blood-bought life.

David Martin

JUST IN TIME

It is a sunny day,
Green leaves softly flutter in the sun,
The flowers open up to God,
His sky above - another day begun.

Suddenly all is black,
Despair envelopes me,
And my body seems to fall, fall, fall
Down into the deep abyss
Oh deep depression - why lean on me?
Why crush out the sweetness of my life?
Other days, I've known happiness
But at this hour all seems amiss.

The walls cram in on me
And pain almost burst my heart
I cannot hear the song of birds.
I only hear the throb
And the deep thudding in my ears and head.

A friend's hand touches mine,
A familiar voice trickles through the void
Like silver water over stones in stream,
And something like refreshment fills my soul.

Someone is listening to my tale of woe
A sympathetic smile wipes away my tears.
Once again I can face the world.
No-one knows what a smile can do.
Only from the depths does its real radiance shine
My God has sent His messages to me -

Just in time.

Margaret R Crooks

GIVE PEACE A CHANCE

Today as I was reading my Bible I stopped to ponder
On the loving words of Jesus and it makes me wonder
We must learn to love was His only command
And forgive each other as we try to understand
We must cast away our fears of the stranger with the gun
As we rise to meet the challenge of a new life with the Son
And when the hatchet's been buried with the loved ones we lost
We must never forget them as we still count the cost
But I pray that in these peace time wounds may start to heal
For I too have faced this task and I know how you feel
So trust in the Father, Son and the Holy Ghost
In these uncertain times it's God we need most
Therefore open your heart to Jesus and He will save you
And close your mind to the demonic words which enslave you
May the Lord bless and protect us as we advance
With hope in our hearts to *give peace a chance.*

Dac C P Doherty

PRAYER

To calmly bow beneath the wing
Of grace in holiness.
To rise and soar, to humbly bring
His wind, to my request.
To sail upon the golden rays
Of His majestic sun.
To stand and shine, to yearn the day
When He, in power, shall come.

William Wade

CHRISTIAN LOVE THEY SAY . . .

Christian love is caring
Christian love is sharing
All the ambitions, hopes and fears
As well as all the problems and tears

Christian love endures
Christian love can cure
Any hurting pain
Without any self-gain

Christian love is perfection
But take what direction?
Lift your eyes above
And see God's holy love

He gave His son
His only one
To die for you and me
That we might be free

For all eternity

Hazel Redmond

SOMEONE

Somewhere out there is a person
who needs my help today,
But will I go to see her
Yes though, perhaps not right away.

I have jobs of my own to see to
And they really must be done.
But oh, that poor old someone
Might expect a visit at home.

Still, I'll just first do my own work
Then when time allows me to
I'll go and visit that old soul
That my friend asked me to.

The housework just keeps on mounting
As the day so quickly flies.
But what about that neighbour
Not to worry, I'll go by and by.

Suddenly, it's school getting out time
And the children are almost here.
My gosh! I have no time left now
To visit that poor old dear.

In sorrow I sit and think, that
I should have gone before
It isn't what God would have wanted
That my house should have come to the fore.

I hope God spares me tomorrow
So that I can obey his call
To visit that frail old someone
Who needed me first of all..

Val Bleakley

I KNOW YOU ARE THERE

When life is busy
And stress wants me to sigh
My soul will take refuge
In God up on high.

When trouble surrounds me
And I'm tested and tried
I know You're my shepherd
You're always by my side.

When I feel lonely
And no-one shows me love
I thank you for sending me
A host from above.

When others desert me
And I'm left on my own
I know You're there for me
I'll never be alone.

You order my steps
My life is in your hands
You placed me on a rock
And secure I now stand.

Amy Blakely

ONLY A WHISPER

When a new life starts to grow inside
and you think to yourself
I've let everyone down.
Abortion is the word that travels in your mind,
Until God whispers to you,
I will be with you, I will never leave you,
nor forsake you.

My heart filled up with a mixture of feelings,
and my eyes just burst with tears
How can you forgive me, after all what
I've done, was my cry
And God answered,
You are still my child.

Nine months later, my baby boy was born
Healthy for all to see,
When I was still in awe with what
a miracle this had been,
And my God had created it all
for me and you.

Lorraine Hodgen

STOP RIPPING THE PAGES

It's so easy to rip out a page of your diary,
To try and forget the past
But does it go away,
Or ever in your memory last.

As we go through life's up and downs,
Do we rip out more paper,
Or simply deny our conscience,
In fear of the reaper.

Loved ones come, loved ones go,
Does your hurt and pain grow,
There's only one love I know,
That never ever goes.

Do you say, not for me, no not I,
And ever refrain from release by cry,
What will it be when your time has come,
Will glory be your kingdom come.

Andrew Campbell

UNTITLED

Have you heard the thunder of the sea?
Have you heard the rustle of leaves on a tree?
Then you have heard God.

Have you glimpsed the smile on a baby's face?
Have you seen a cobweb that's finer than lace?
Then you have seen God.

Have you felt the tender touch of a
mother's love?
Have you stroked the feathers on the back
of a dove?
Then you have felt God.

Have you smelt the perfume of the rose?
Have you tasted food when hunger goes?
Then you have had a taste of God.

Have you been touched by loving hands?
Be they a woman's or a man's
Then you have been touched by God.

Kathleen McManus

PRAYER

Guide our hands, Oh Lord and King
Let our hymns your praises sing,
Let us see by deed and word
The pen is stronger than the sword.

Let not our lips speak hasty words,
Think well of others be not cowards;
Let our ears heed not the lie
Spread by rumour let it die.

Take the scales from off our eyes
So we may see your heaven above,
As each day passes each day flies,
Show us the answer is with love.

Guide our steps that we may see
The path to follow led by thee;
Then we will not be afraid
As darkness falls and on we tread.

Annette Gordon

THANKSGIVING

Father God, I cannot comprehend your
mighty power.
But I've learned to lean on You
For strength from hour to hour.
I've prayed to You for healing,
Knowing You still have control.
I've yielded my life completely.
Searched my very heart and soul..
You've heard my cry for mercy,
You've carried me each day
You've given me a peace of mind,
No-one can take away!
You've proved beyond all measure
That You are alive in me.
Your miracles still happen . . .
They're not just for Calvary!
We must not try and limit Your
authority and power,
But accept that we alone must trust
In You from hour to hour
As You fill us with Your spirit
We learn to love You more . . .
To give You thanks and praise You
Makes our earthly bodies soar,
Above the little worries, above all
hurt and pain,
Sharing sweet communion with our
Saviour once again
And lifted above the trials,
We focus Lord on You.
And feel Your love enfold us
As Your spirit surges through.

Daphne Henning

YOUR CHILDREN

Lord your little children
How much you love them so
As they play around together
You are with them as they go
You show them fun and laughter
And watch them jump for joy
How much you love your children Lord
Every girl and every boy.

Wendy P Adams

THE DREAM

I dreamed I stood upon a spot
Of barren time and space.
It was a woeful wilderness
Where thistles grew apace,
And all around it ran a wall,
That scale I'd never dare,
For on its other side, I knew,
Lay darkness and despair.

I dreamed I saw the self same spot
But what a change I found!
Instead of thistles roses bloomed
In cultivated ground.
I walked through marble palaces,
Through rooms fair to behold,
All filled with storied tapestries
And porcelain and gold.

A voice cried, 'Think of what you've seen
And then go tend your plot,
For it, with just some industry
Can be what it is not.
So quarry marble, mine your gold,
So dig your land, plant flowers,
Go fire your vases, work your scenes,
For you have place and hours.'

V M Archer

THE SABBATH DAY

The Sabbath is a special day
A day of peace and rest.
A blessed day, a family day
A day that is the best
The public worship and the prayers
The loud sweet songs of praise
The family prayers that thrills the heart
With joy and pleasure raise.

What would the world be like? I say, without the Sabbath day.
A garden without flowers, a meadow without hay
A rainbow without colours, night skies without bright stars
The Sabbath day a jewel is with wealth and joy by far.

God in his goodness man did make.
He knew what strain that man could take.
And so he made the Sabbath rest, for man's
weak frame this was the best.
God gave to man six other days, that he could
spend in many ways.
But on the Sabbath, holy keep, a special day
in all the week.

James McIlhatton

INFORMATION

We hope you have enjoyed reading this book - and that you will continue to enjoy it in the coming years.

If you like reading and writing poetry drop us a line, or give us a call, and we'll send you a free information pack.

Write to

Triumph House Information
1-2 Wainman Road
Woodston
Peterborough
PE2 7BU